MONSTERS in MYTH

THE MINOTAUR

MONSTERS in MYTH

TITLES IN THE SERIES

MONSTERS in MYTH

THE MINOTAUR

RUSSELL ROBERTS

Mitchell Lane
PUBLISHERS
P.O. BOX 196
HOCKESSIN, DELAWARE 19707
VISIT US ON THE WEB: WWW.MITCHELLLANE.COM
COMMENTS? EMAIL US: MITCHELLLANE@MITCHELLLANE.COM

Printing   2   3   4   5   6   7   8   9

Library of Congress Cataloging-in-Publication Data
Roberts, Russell, 1953–
   The minotaur / by Russell Roberts.
       p. cm. — (Monsters in myth)
   Includes bibliographical references and index.
   ISBN 978-1-58415-929-2 (library bound)
   1. Minotaur (Greek mythology)—Juvenile literature. 1. Title.
   BL820.M63R63 2010
   398.20938'01—dc22
                                                                                    2010006557

ABOUT THE AUTHOR: Russell Roberts has written and published nearly 40 books for adults and children on a variety of subjects, including baseball, memory power, business, New Jersey history, and travel. He has written numerous books for Mitchell Lane Publishers, including *Nathaniel Hawthorne, Holidays and Celebrations in Colonial America, What's So Great About Daniel Boone, The Life and Times of Nostradamus, Poseidon,* and *The Cyclopes.* He lives in Bordentown, New Jersey, with his family and a fat, fuzzy, and crafty calico cat named Rusti.

AUTHOR'S NOTE: Portions of this story have been retold using dialogue as an aid to readability. The dialogue is based on the author's extensive research and approximates what might have occurred at the time.

PUBLISHER'S NOTE: This story is based on the author's extensive research, which he believes to be accurate. Documentation of such research is contained on page 46.
        The internet sites referenced herein were active as of the publication date. Due to the fleeting nature of some web sites, we cannot guarantee they will all be active when you are reading this book.
        To reflect current usage, we have chosen to use the secular era designations BCE ("before the common era") and CE ("of the common era") instead of the traditional designations BC ("before Christ") and AD (*anno Domini,* "in the year of the Lord").

TABLE OF CONTENTS

MONSTERS IN MYTH

MINOTAUR

The fearsome Minotaur continues to fascinate artists and storytellers. A sand sculpture of the Minotaur at the World Sand Castle Championships in Harrison Hot Springs Resort and Spa in British Columbia, Canada, glowers at its audience.

MINOTAUR

CHAPTER 1

Hunting Evil

The young man walked slowly, haltingly, through dim stone passageways that were illuminated only by the flickering light of an occasional torch fastened to the wall. Sometimes he stumbled and almost fell onto the hard dirt floor. Only by sticking his hand out to grasp the wall could he avoid falling. In the near-total blackness, he kept wondering: How do I know what I'm grabbing? I can't see a thing! Then an even scarier thought would pass through him, sending a shiver down his spine: What if the horrible, flesh-eating Minotaur (MIH-nuh-tar) is right in front of me and I can't see it? What do I do then? What if it grabs me and rips me to pieces before I even see it? All he had to defend himself were his fists—and a ball of thread.

The young man, Theseus (THEE-see-us), was from the Greek city of Athens. He had come to the island nation of Crete to try to stop a terrible wrong—the yearly killing of seven young men and seven young women by the awful half-bull, half-human creature known as the Minotaur. The only way he could do that was to kill the beast.

Killing the Minotaur would not be easy. It lived here, in a world of winding, confusing, interconnecting passageways called the Labyrinth. A clever master builder named Daedalus (DEH-duh-lus) had designed it with so many twists and turns to make it impossible for the Minotaur to ever escape. But the maze worked both ways. While the creature could never escape, humans who entered the Labyrinth could never figure out how to get out of it, either. Eventually the ferocious Minotaur would find them and devour them.

CHAPTER 1

Theseus heard a sound! What was it? He peered through the blackness, trying to see through the curtain of darkness. But try as he might, he could see nothing. Was it the fearful Minotaur that he had heard?

Fearful indeed was the horrible Minotaur. It had the head and tail of a bull on the body of a man. Once it found people wandering in its Labyrinth, it quickly killed and ate them, leaving nothing but bones. Sometimes, by the light of the torches on the wall, Theseus would see piles of bones, and he knew they marked yet another victim of the Minotaur.

Theseus knew all this, and yet he hoped that he would be able to find the Minotaur—before it found him—and kill it. Even more surprising was that Theseus had volunteered for this terribly dangerous task. He had willingly allowed himself to be placed into the bewildering Labyrinth in search of the beast.

Why had he put himself into such grave danger? The answer was easy: It was the only way to stop the continuing slaughter of innocent Athenian youths who were being sacrificed to the Minotaur.

Some time before Theseus arrived, King Minos (MEE-nos) of Crete had attacked Athens. Crete was very powerful, and it had defeated Athens. The cruel king had decreed that Athens must send seven young men and seven young maidens each year to be fed to the Minotaur. Athens had to comply.

Theseus was appalled when he heard this story. He knew the Minotaur had to be stopped, and that the Athenian sacrifices must end. This year, he had volunteered to come as one of the fourteen.

There! There was that snuffling sound again! What could it be? Theseus looked around, his head swiveling from side to side, but he could see nothing in this maze. It was too dark—too gloomy. He could barely see his hand in front of his face. But he could smell an odor, and it was slowly getting stronger. It was the stench of decaying flesh. He must be getting close to the Minotaur. Theseus shuddered as he saw more stacks of victims' bones lying on the ground all around him.

Nineteenth-century artist Sir Edward Burne-Jones depicts Theseus with a sword. Burne-Jones designed this illustration for use on a ceramic tile—something the artist did often.

Would he be the Minotaur's next victim? Thoughts raced through his head of all that he had gone through to find his father, and how he had faced danger—and even death—so many times before finally reuniting with him. He also thought about the treachery of his father's second wife, and how she had almost caused his death.

He looked down at the ball of thread in his hand and remembered the beautiful Ariadne (ayr-ee-AD-nee), King Minos's daughter. She had seen him when the sacrifices from Athens were paraded before the king, and had fallen in love with him. Ariadne had decided to save Theseus from the Minotaur, so she had given him the ball of thread and explained her plan to him. But would he live to carry it out?

Theseus turned a corner. Suddenly, standing not more than ten feet away, was the Minotaur. The creature glared at Theseus; its nostrils flared, and from its throat came a blood-chilling scream. Its horns gleamed in the light from a nearby torch.

Theseus's feet froze. He stood rooted to the spot, staring at the ferocious beast in front of him. The Minotaur tilted its head slightly, giving Theseus a full view of its two sharp horns and its mouthful of jagged teeth. Slowly the loathsome beast began coming toward Theseus. It stretched its claws out, ready to grab the young man in its powerful arms.

Theseus took a few steps backward. The Minotaur looked at his prey hungrily; there was murder in its eyes. Bellowing, the Minotaur closed in on Theseus for the kill.

Minotaur, Yorkshire Sculpture Park, England

Crete in the Ancient World

Crete is the largest island in modern Greece, and the fifth-largest island in the Mediterranean Sea, covering a distance of over 3,200 square miles (8,300 square kilometers). During ancient times, Crete was a major power and played an important role in Greek history.

Crete was the home of one of the earliest civilizations in European history. Its most legendary and prosperous period was known as the Minoan, named after the fabled King Minos. It is thought that this period lasted from about 2600 to 1200 BCE.

Many tales are concerned with King Minos. Although he is portrayed as evil in the Minotaur story, he is supposed to have been wise and just. Some Greek myths identify Crete as the island on which Zeus, king of the gods, was raised. The most popular myth to take place on Crete was that of the Minotaur.

One reason Crete was so prosperous is that its citizens maintained a vigorous trade with other regions. Crete traded in olive oil, cereals, and wine. This prosperity enabled them to develop towns with cisterns (tanks for storing water), pathways, and sewage systems. Their bustling trade with others also helped them develop a superb fleet of ships, and Crete's sea power helped it maintain its political strength.

It is believed that ancient Crete was the first Greek region to develop writing. Modern archaeological excavations on the island have uncovered stones containing an early form of writing called Linear A, which has yet to be deciphered.[1] Along with writing, Crete during the Minoan era is also thought to have invented a system of currency.

Crete flourished until around 1500 or 1600 BCE. At that time, it is believed, a volcanic eruption on nearby Santorini caused tsunamis that destroyed parts of the civilization that existed on Crete. Other theories about the civilization's decline involve deforestation and invasion. The Cretans were eventually conquered by the Mycenaens.

King Minos judges a condemned soul in an illustration for *Inferno*, the first part of the epic poem *Divine Comedy* by Dante Alighieri. The illustration was created by the French artist Gustave Doré.

MINOTAUR

CHAPTER 2

The Tale of Two Kings

The story of how the Minotaur came to be is, first and foremost, the story of King Minos of Crete. However, Greek myth portrays Minos in two dissimilar lights: good and wise, then evil and vindictive. Which Minos starred in the story of the Minotaur? Were both kings one and the same? Or were there two kings named Minos?

(Before you decide, remember that Greek myths were not meant to be read together like a novel, with a distinct beginning, middle, and end. The Greek tales frequently contradict one another.)

According to the stories, Minos was one of three male children fathered on the island of Crete by Zeus, the king of the gods, with a woman named Europa (yoo-ROH-puh). These children were Minos, Rhadamanthys (rad-uh-MAN-this), and Sarpedon (SAR-peh-don).[1] After Zeus left her, Europa married Asterius, who was king of Crete at that time.

When the marriage of Europa and Asterius proved to be childless, the king adopted Minos, Rhadamanthys, and Sarpedon. Asterius was very kind, and he treated the three boys with love and respect. The youths grew up happily in the fabulous palace of Knossos (NOH-sus) on Crete.

As brothers often do, the three argued. The reason for the argument is often not given. However, Greek mythology expert Robert Graves writes, "They quarreled for the love of a beautiful boy named Miletus."[2] Miletus (my-LEE-tus) eventually decided that he wanted to be with Sarpedon. This infuriated Minos, who drove Miletus from Crete. (Do not feel too bad for Miletus. According to Graves, he sailed to a place called Caria in Asia Minor, where he founded the city and kingdom of Miletus.)[3]

Another version of the story has Minos suspecting Miletus of trying to overthrow him and seize the kingdom. However, Miletus apparently had a special relationship with Apollo, god of light. Minos did not want to anger the god and thus could do nothing but tell Miletus that he knew of his plan, whereby Miletus escaped to Caria on his own.[4]

No matter what version is followed, Minos became king of Crete. There, it is said, he conversed with Zeus for either nine years or every nine years. He received the laws for his kingdom directly from Zeus. The laws—and thus Minos himself—were celebrated for being wise and just. He also developed the constitution for Crete.

Because he was so respected by the gods for his wisdom, the myths say that when he died, Minos was made a judge of the dead in the Underworld. According to the story, two other judges had votes, with Minos casting the final and tiebreaking one. (One of the two other judges was Rhadamanthys.)

Some say that Minos had a son, and that this son subsequently had a son named Minos, named after his grandfather. This King Minos, it is said, was the "bad" king who demanded sacrifices from Athens to feed to the Minotaur. As Greek myth researcher Félix Guirand writes, "It seems, however, that we should distinguish at least two kings called Minos, of which one was the grandson of the other."[5]

Is this how Minos went from "good" to "bad"? Were there two kings named Minos? Or was there only one? Graves draws a straight line from the Minos fathered by Zeus to the circumstances that led to the arrival of the Minotaur.[6] Were the "bad" and "good" kings always the same person? Some researchers believe that *Minos* was not even a real name, but rather a hereditary title given to all the kings of Crete.[7]

Minos is certainly an important person in the history of the ancient world. In fact, the time period is called "the Minoan" after Minos. But who was he really? Researchers still ponder this question.

No matter how it happened, when Minos became king, the chain of events that would bring forth the dreadful Minotaur began to unfold.

Minos was crowned after much controversy and competition for the throne. Even after he was monarch, he faced questions about whether he was the right person to be ruler. In order to quiet the doubters, he boasted that he was in so much favor with the gods that they would answer whatever prayer he offered to them.

"I am the gods' choice for this throne, their favorite, and to prove it, I will show you that they will grant any request that I make of them," he said.

Once he had made the statement, of course, he had to back it up. He built an altar near the shore and dedicated it to Poseidon (poh-SY-dun), the god of the sea, in order to gain favor with him. He then got down on his knees and prayed to the god that a bull would emerge from the sea.

"O great Poseidon, lord of the seas, master of the waves, the winds, and the waters, please send a bull to me to show that I am in your favor," he said. "If you do, I will sacrifice it in your honor on this magnificent altar that I have built as a tribute to you."

Minos had just finished his prayer when the sea parted. Out of the gap emerged a magnificent white bull—the most splendid creature Minos had ever seen. Poseidon had answered the king's request in a most spectacular way.

No sooner had Minos laid eyes on the white bull than he began to think of reasons *not* to keep his promise to Poseidon. It was a superb animal, the king thought. It would be a shame to kill it. Instead, Minos decided to spare the white bull and let it join his own herd. He picked another bull to sacrifice to Poseidon in place of the white one. After all, the king reasoned, he was still sacrificing a bull to Poseidon—just not that one.

But it mattered to Poseidon. The god had sent that particular animal to Minos because the king had said he would sacrifice it in the god's honor. That was why the animal had been so impressive. The god had sent a wonderful animal, and now Minos had broken his promise. Poseidon—always a bit of a cranky god—was not pleased.

For the moment, Minos had achieved his purpose. With the arrival of the bull, the islanders accepted him as their true king—everyone except Sarpedon. Angry, Minos expelled him from Crete. Sarpedon traveled to Cilicia (now part of southern Turkey), where he eventually became king.[8]

Meanwhile, Minos had married a woman named Pasiphae (PAS-ih-fay). Poseidon saw his chance to get revenge on Minos. He made Pasiphae fall madly in love with the white bull. Being with the animal was all she could think about. But how could she satisfy her craving? There was only one person who could help her: Daedalus, the clever craftsman and inventor.

Pasiphae went to the craftsman and confessed her desire for the white bull. How could she fulfill that desire? Would he help her?

"I will, my queen," Daedalus promised.

Since the white bull was grazing in a field with Minos's other bulls, Daedalus knew that Pasiphae would have to sneak up on it without scaring the others and starting a stampede. He built a hollow wooden cow on wheels and covered it with cowhide. The other cows would think it was just another cow and ignore it. Daedalus wheeled it into the meadow where the white bull was grazing and showed Pasiphae how to operate it.[9]

Pasiphae did exactly as Daedalus had told her. Sure enough, after the queen had waited in the field awhile inside the hollow cow, the white bull came up and spent time with her. Pasiphae's desire was fulfilled.

This encounter was just the beginning. The bull had sired a child with Pasiphae. When she gave birth, her baby was a hideous creature that was half man and half bull: the Minotaur.

There are other versions of the story. Some say that Minos had offended Poseidon because the king had sacrificed his best bull to the god every year, and one year he sacrificed a lesser animal rather than his best. Sometimes it is said that the god he offended was not Poseidon, but Zeus. Still others say that it was Aphrodite (af-roh-DY-tee), the goddess of love and beauty, who was offended, and not by Minos, but by Pasiphae. It was Aphrodite who made the queen crave the bull.

In a wall painting found in the ruins of Pompeii, the master builder and inventor Daedalus explains to Pasiphae how to use the mechanical bull.

Pasiphae and her infant son the Minotaur are featured on a fourth-century BCE kylix.

The magnificent white bull had no luck either. It grew savage and wild after being with Pasiphae, and eventually Heracles (HAYR-uh-kleez), also known as Hercules (HER-kyoo-leez), captured it and brought it to Athens.

At first, Minos and Pasiphae tried to raise their mutant offspring in secret, but as the creature grew older it became more unruly, and Minos knew that something had to be done. He consulted an oracle to find out how he could best avoid scandal and hide his wife's shame. An oracle was a priestess to a god, considered to have great knowledge because it was thought the god spoke through her. "Have Daedalus build you a retreat at Knossos," said the oracle.[10]

Minos followed these instructions, and Daedalus built the winding, bewildering Labyrinth. Sometimes the Labyrinth is considered a separate place all its own. However, as Graves writes, "Minos spent the remainder of his life in the inextricable maze called the Labyrinth, at the very heart of which he concealed Pasiphae and the Minotaur."[11]

This would indicate that the Labyrinth was not a separate place that housed only the Minotaur, but that it was part of the palace where Minos lived. Experts still debate whether this is true.

Once the Minotaur was safely inside the Labyrinth, Minos had to figure out how to feed it.

Poseidon

It is not surprising that Poseidon was the trigger for the birth of the Minotaur. Of all the Greek gods, he is possibly the crankiest and surliest, and he has a close connection with bulls.

Poseidon was one of the children of Gaia (GY-uh) and Kronos (KROH-nus). Kronos swallowed each of his children as they were born so that none of them could become powerful enough to overthrow him. Ultimately Gaia spirited away one child—Zeus—before Kronos could find him and swallow him. Zeus grew up and decided to fight his father. First, he and his mother tricked Kronos into drinking mustard and vinegar, causing him to vomit up all the children, including Poseidon. The full-grown children then fought Kronos and the other Titans for control of the universe. After their victory, Zeus and his brothers divided the world. Zeus was king of the gods and sky, Poseidon god of the sea, and Hades (HAY-deez) god of the Underworld.

Poseidon lived in a palace made of coral and gemstones on the ocean floor. He drove a magnificent chariot that could ride on the water. He carried a large trident with which he could do immense damage.

Mariners prayed to Poseidon, for it was his temperament that dictated whether or not a voyage would be safe. When he was in a good mood, he provided sailors with calm seas. When agitated or disturbed, however, he would cause rough seas and violent weather. When he struck the ground with his trident he caused earthquakes, which could result in massive waves.

Poseidon could be a fearsome god. After he lost a contest with Athena for who would become the patron god of Athens, he sent a terrible flood to the city. Angry with Odysseus for blinding his son Polyphemus, the Cyclops, he sent storms that blew the Greeks off course and kept them from reaching home for ten years. Their quest is told in Homer's *Odyssey*.

Like Zeus, Poseidon had many love affairs. One of the most notorious was when he pursued the goddess Demeter, who turned herself into a mare to escape him. Poseidon turned himself into a stallion and caught her. To Poseidon, Demeter bore the goddess Despoina (des-POH-ih-nah) and the immortal horse Areion (AYR-ee-on). Another of Poseidon's affairs supposedly resulted in the birth of the mighty Theseus, though his father may have been Aegeus, king of Athens.

As his mother looks on, Theseus lifts a stone to find sandals and a sword left there for him by his father, Aegeus.

MINOTAUR

Theseus the Hero

Although Theseus was just a young man when he faced the Minotaur, he was already a hero in Athens. His mother, Aethra (or Aithra—ETH-ruh), was the daughter of Pittheus (PIH-thee-us), the king of Troezen. She was married to Aegeus (or Aigeus—EE-jee-us), the king of Athens. There is some question about who the real father of Theseus was: some say it was Aegeus, and some say it was Poseidon. Either way, after Theseus was born, Aegeus was worried that his nephews would try to murder him.[1] He left Aethra with her father in Troezen to bring up the boy. Before he returned to Athens, Aegeus placed a sword and a pair of sandals under a giant rock.

"When Theseus is strong enough to lift this rock and take the sword and sandals from beneath it, he should be allowed to travel to Athens to find his father," Aegeus said.

Theseus grew up brave and strong, and the day came when his mother took him to the great rock and instructed him to try to lift it. The boy was puzzled about his mother's request, but he obeyed her wishes. He easily lifted the rock. There beneath it were the sword and sandals, just as Aegeus had left them years before.

"Mother!" the boy cried. "What does this mean?"

Aethra explained what Aegeus had said and done, and Theseus resolved to set out for Athens immediately. But both Aethra and Pittheus voiced concern.

"The road to Athens is filled with bandits, thieves, and murderers," said the king. "It would be best if you went by ship."

"No," replied the boy. "I want to face the dangers of the road, just as Heracles once did. Perhaps if I can defeat these ruffians, I can win renown the same as the great hero."

Soon after Theseus set off for Athens, he met the bandit Periph-etes (per-IH-feh-teez), who attacked him with a huge club. Theseus wrestled the club away from his attacker and killed him with it. This became the pattern of every hazard Theseus faced along the way: He defeated his opponent with the opponent's own weapon.

His next adversary would tear unwary travelers to pieces by tying their limbs to pine trees he had bent down, then letting the trees

The trip to Athens was very dangerous for Theseus. The road was filled with bandits who would lie in wait to attack—including Sinis, the Pine-Bender.

snap back. Theseus did the same to him. Another foe tried to kick the young man into the sea, but wound up getting thrown there himself. Another, Procrustes (proh-KRUS-teez) tried to murder Theseus in a specially designed bed, but it was he who died in the bed rather than Theseus. All other enemies Theseus encountered on the road met their end as well.

News travels fast, and by the time Theseus reached Athens, he was a hero for defeating all the bandits.[2] King Aegeus did not recognize him as his son, for he was under the spell of the sorceress Medea (meh-DEE-uh), who some say was his wife, and Theseus did not reveal himself to the king. Medea plotted to get rid of Theseus by asking him to kill the Bull of Marathon, whom Heracles had brought to Athens from Crete.[3] This was the same magnificent white bull that Poseidon had sent to Minos, and who had fathered the Minotaur. The bull had turned into a fierce creature, breathing smoke and fire from its nostrils. It had been terrorizing the countryside of Athens. Theseus defeated it.

Once that plot failed, Medea planned to kill Theseus by poisoning him at a banquet given in his honor. (Another version says Aegeus was worried that the young man would become popular enough that the people would make him king in place of Aegeus, so he consented to a plan by Medea to poison him.[4]) Either way, when Theseus arrived at the banquet, Medea handed him a cup of poisoned wine.

"Please partake of some refreshment, mighty stranger," said Medea, with a smile that masked her true intentions.

Theseus accepted the cup. Before he put it to his lips, he drew the sword that he had taken from under the giant rock.

"That sword!" gasped Aegeus, instantly recognizing it as the one he had left for his son many years before. If he had been under a spell, the sight of the sword broke it. Aegeus leaped to his feet and knocked the cup of wine from Theseus's hand just before he took a drink. The wine boiled and hissed as it ran over the stones in the

ground, and the king realized that Medea had tried to poison his son. She fled for her life, and father and son were joyfully reunited.

The reunion was short-lived, for once again Aegeus looked troubled.

The evil Medea offers Theseus poisoned wine in this 1910 painting by W. Russell Flint. Aegeus, next to Theseus, seems to be in a trance.

"What is the matter, my father?" asked Theseus.

The worried king replied, "We Athenians are the victims of a terrible tribute that must be paid to King Minos of Crete. Some time ago the son of Minos, Androgeus [an-DROH-jee-us], came to Athens to visit me. He was a fine, strapping youth. One day he noticed me looking concerned, and asked me why. I told him that the Bull of Marathon was wreaking havoc in the countryside. I said I would give anything for that foul creature to be destroyed. Androgeus looked at me and said, 'I will do it. I will kill the Bull of Marathon.' By the gods, I thought that he could, and so I let him go forth." (Other myths say that the king sent Androgeus in search of the bull, hoping the boy would be killed.)

Aegeus looked at Theseus with a tortured expression. "I should have never let him go. But I did, and the Bull of Marathon killed him. When Minos heard about it, he was sick with grief and vowed vengeance. So he attacked Athens." The king buried his face in his hands.

Theseus quietly listened to his father. When the king was calm, the youth gently asked, "What happened then, my father?"

Defiantly, the king looked up at his son. "We fought. We resisted. Minos could not defeat Athens, so he started a siege, which too dragged on and on. Finally, in desperation, he asked the help of Zeus. Zeus sent a plague down upon us to further add to our miseries.[5] So we went to the oracle of Apollo and asked what we should do. She said we should make peace with Minos and accede to his demands."

The king's shoulders sagged. "To rid ourselves of this plague, and the siege, we agreed to send seven male youths and seven maidens every year to be fed to that dreadful creature, the Minotaur.[6] Now that terrible time has come again, when fourteen of our finest young men and women must be sent to die at the hands of this creature."

(Some sources say that the fourteen men and women to be sacrificed were sent to the Minotaur every nine years.)

When he was certain that his father had finished, Theseus said quietly, "I will go to Crete as one of the fourteen to be sacrificed, and I will slay the Minotaur and free Athens from this curse forever."

When the time came for lots to be drawn to see which youths were to be sent to Crete as sacrifices, Theseus stepped forward and said: "People of Athens, it is not right that your children should go and that I, who am the son of King Aegeus, should remain behind. Surely, if any of the youths of Athens should face the dread monster of Crete, I should face it. There is one lot that you may leave undrawn. I will go to Crete."[7]

When Theseus heard the story of the Minotaur, he volunteered to try to free the people of Athens from this monster.

Aegeus begged his son to reconsider. He knew no one had survived in the Labyrinth of the Minotaur. But Theseus was firm, and finally his father agreed to let him go.

The ship carrying the fourteen sacrifices to Crete always flew black sails—the color of death. Before it left Athens, Aegeus gave it a white sail as well, and instructed Theseus to sail that one when the ship returned if he was successful in killing the Minotaur. If, however, Theseus was unsuccessful, the ship was to sail its usual black sail, and Aegeus would know that the Minotaur had defeated Theseus.

Travel in Ancient Greece

Aethra and Pittheus were right to warn Theseus against walking to Athens. Traveling by foot in ancient Greece was both dangerous and challenging.

Horseback riding was not popular, as only the very rich had horses. Neither stirrups nor saddles were known, so riding was done bareback—an undertaking that quickly became painful.

Chariots and other vehicles that used wheels were good for only short distances as well. Thus there were two main modes of travel in ancient Greece: by foot or by boat. Each came with its own difficulties.

Walking was common for Greeks, and walking or running long distances over several days' time was just part of life. The roads were dangerous, however, because thieves, bandits, and murderers could easily attack innocent travelers. In addition, there was not a vast complex of roads for travelers to use; roads were local, and they did not always link one community to another. Thus, those traveling long distances inevitably had to travel over rough, rocky terrain, and try to keep their sense of direction about them.

The most common method of travel in ancient Greece was by sea—Greece has no rivers large enough to navigate by ship. However, both the weather and frequent attacks by pirates made sea travel just as dangerous as walking.

In Homer's *Odyssey*, Poseidon conjures up the rough seas and bad weather that shipwrecks Odysseus's fleet and keeps the hero from arriving home for ten years. Some feel that the story is a reflection of the ancient Greeks' fear of sea travel.

A palace at Knossos. King Minos of Crete lived in a spectacular palace. Some modern experts believe that the palace itself could have been the famous Labyrinth.

MINOTAUR

CHAPTER 4

Fight to the Death!

Theseus sailed with the thirteen other young men and women who had been selected by lot to be sacrificed to the Minotaur. The others were very scared, but when they looked at Theseus on the deck of the ship, they had a glimmer of hope. Maybe, by some miracle, he could save them.

When the ship sailed into the harbor of Knossos and the other youths from Athens saw King Minos's palace, they shrank back in terror. They knew that the deadly Labyrinth was here also, and that the Minotaur was waiting there. Meanwhile Theseus looked all about him, taking in as much of the area as possible, planning his next move.

The youths were brought before Minos. As he and others of his court observed the fourteen, Theseus stood out for the firm way he stared back at the king. Ariadne, the daughter of Minos, was also watching the group. Minos called a contest between Theseus and the best wrestler in Crete. When Theseus defeated the other man before all who watched him in the palace, Ariadne fell in love with him.

That night Ariadne came to Theseus and offered to help him escape the Minotaur—but she would not help the others. Theseus refused to leave the other youths to their fate, so the princess came up with another plan. She had gone to Daedalus and begged him to help her save Theseus. He told her what to do, and Ariadne gave the secret of the Labyrinth to Theseus: a ball of thread.

Some also say that Theseus asked Ariadne to get the sword back for him that the Cretan guards had taken when he had arrived on the

Ariadne tells Theseus the secret to escaping the Labyrinth. Fortunately for Theseus, before he was sent to the Labyrinth, Ariadne saw him and fell in love with him.

island. Others make no mention of Theseus having any weapon but his fists when he entered the Labyrinth.

Either way, the next day, just as Theseus entered the Labyrinth, he tied one end of the ball of thread inside the door. He then unwound the thread as he walked through the twisting passageways. Theseus would thus be able to follow the thread back to the entrance, perfectly retracing his steps so that he would not get confused and become lost.

Trailing his thread, Theseus faced the horrible Minotaur. The creature closed in on the hero, slobbering and howling. Its powerful hands opened and closed, and Theseus knew that if the creature grabbed him it might easily crush him. With a bloodcurdling cry, the

Minotaur slashed at Theseus. The man darted away, and the creature screamed in frustration.

As the Minotaur glared at Theseus, the hero stared back defiantly. The Minotaur roared, its horrible tongue lolling out of one side of its mouth as it screamed. The sound jolted Theseus into action. Fury boiled inside him, and he leaped at the monster.

The two locked in combat. The Minotaur tried to tear at Theseus with its long claws and bite him with its razor-sharp teeth. Theseus struggled to avoid these weapons as he sought to gain the advantage on the creature. He could feel the Minotaur's hot breath on his neck as the beast strained to bite him. Its claws tore at his skin. Theseus was stronger than most, but he felt the creature's powerful arms winding around his body in a fatal crush.

For a few minutes the outlook was uncertain. Suddenly the Minotaur relaxed its grip and slumped to the ground. The Minotaur was dead. Some say Theseus strangled him with his bare hands. Artwork shows him using a sword, spear, or club to crush its skull.

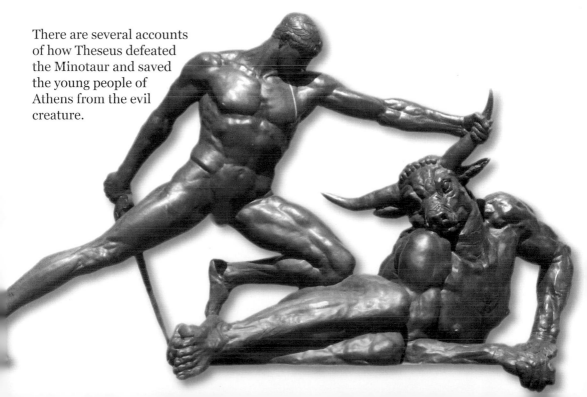

There are several accounts of how Theseus defeated the Minotaur and saved the young people of Athens from the evil creature.

Breathing heavily, bleeding from the places where the Minotaur had gashed him, his body drenched with perspiration, Theseus reached down and picked up the ball of thread he had dropped. Ariadne's plan worked perfectly; the youth followed the thread back out to the opening of the Labyrinth. Once he was outside and people saw him, word quickly spread: Theseus had killed the Minotaur.

When Minos learned that Daedalus had helped Ariadne solve the secret of the Labyrinth, thus enabling Theseus to kill the Minotaur and come out of the Labyrinth alive, he was furious. He locked Daedalus and his son Icarus (IH-kuh-rus) into the Labyrinth, and told Ariadne that she was no longer welcome in his palace.

"I helped you escape the Labyrinth and kill the Minotaur," Ariadne said to Theseus. "Take me back to Athens with you and make me your wife."

Theseus, realizing how much she had helped him, agreed. (Some say that Ariadne gleaned the marriage promise before she gave him the ball of thread.)

Theseus and the other young Athenians, who could scarcely believe their good fortune in having escaped certain death at the hands of the Minotaur, boarded their ship to return to Athens.

For some, this was the end of the Minotaur saga. But for others, the tale would continue.

Theseus cut holes in the bottom of all the Cretan ships so that they filled with water and thus could not chase the Athenians as they sailed home.[1] They started their journey, then anchored at the island of Naxos. However, while everyone slept on shore that night, Theseus and the rest of the Athenians soundlessly boarded the ship. In the morning, when Ariadne awoke, the ship—and Theseus—were gone.

Why did he abandon her? Some say the gods told him to do so in a dream, while others say that he did not want to take a foreign-born wife back to Athens. Still others say it was all a mistake, and that Theseus never meant to leave her there.[2] But left behind she was, and she cried bitterly over her fate.

Things did not go too badly for Ariadne, however. Later that day a ship came to Naxos that carried the god Dionysus. When the two saw each other they instantly fell in love, and remained with each other forever.

Possibly preoccupied with thoughts of Ariadne, Theseus forgot to change the black sail to white as the ship approached Athens. King

Even heroes aren't perfect! On his return to Athens, Theseus forgot to change the black sail on his ship to white, a signal to his father, King Aegeus, that he was still alive.

Aegeus had been anxiously watching for the ship's return. Now he saw it approach, and saw that the sail was still black, and thought that the Minotaur had killed his son. In despair he threw himself off a cliff into the sea that now bears his name—the Aegean Sea.

Theseus became king of Athens, but he soon stepped down from the throne because he thought it better if the people ruled themselves. Thus Athens became one of the greatest cities in the world, a democracy, where the people governed themselves. The Athenians coined the phrase "Nothing Without Theseus" to always remember his role in Athens' greatness. [3]

The story did not end well for Minos. Already furious at Daedalus, he was even more incensed when the inventor escaped from the Labyrinth. The king summoned Crete's awesome shipping power and set off after Daedalus.

Minos did not know where Daedalus had gone. However, he brought a puzzle with him. Everywhere he stopped, he promised to reward anyone who could pass a string through a shell. When he landed in Sicily, he gave the shell to Kokalos, the king of Kamikos. Kokalos secretly gave the shell to Daedalus, who threaded the shell and returned it to the king. When Kokalos handed the shell back to Minos, the king knew that Daedalus was in Kamikos. Only Daedalus could have solved the puzzle. Minos demanded that Kokalos surrender Daedalus to him.

However, the daughters of Kokalos did not want to lose Daedalus, who made them beautiful toys. [4] They, along with Daedalus, hatched a plan to kill Minos. Using a pipe, they poured either boiling oil or water onto the king as he bathed, killing him. [5] Then as the Greek historian Herodotus wrote: "After the death of Minos, the Cretans fell into total disorder." [6] The nation of Crete never recovered from the death of their mighty king, and declined as a world power.

Daedalus and Icarus

Although he was a mortal and not a god or hero, Daedalus is one of the most famous figures in Greek mythology. Not only did he create the Labyrinth for holding the Minotaur and the fake bull for Pasiphae, he also had a fanciful adventure with his son, Icarus.

Daedalus was originally from Athens, where he gained a reputation as an architect, inventor, and craftsman. For a time he took in his sister's son Perdix as his apprentice. Perdix was intelligent, and Daedalus became fearful that the boy would one day surpass his accomplishments. He murdered Perdix by throwing him off a cliff. For this, Daedalus was exiled from Athens.

He wound up in Crete, where he again gained a reputation as a clever builder and inventor. Pasiphae asked him to help her be with the white bull, and King Minos asked him to build the Labyrinth. However, the inventor wound up in his own invention when Minos learned of Daedalus's involvement with Theseus and Ariadne. Furious, the king locked Daedalus and Icarus in the Labyrinth.

The king had not reckoned on Daedalus's ingenuity. The inventor made a set of wings for him and his son out of wax, feathers, and reeds. He warned Icarus to fly at a medium height: too low and the sea would dampen the feathers and make them too heavy; too high and the sun would melt the wax.

The wings worked perfectly, and the two were able to escape the Labyrinth. However, Icarus forgot his father's warning and flew too close to the sun. The wax holding his feathers melted, and Icarus plunged into the sea and drowned. That sea is called the Icarian Sea. Daedalus went on to live in Sicily.

From this story we get the expression "flew too close to the sun," which usually means someone attempted something too ambitious and failed.

Daedalus and Icarus, a painting by Lord Frederick Leighton

A Minotaur statue made of wire. Even though the story of the Minotaur took place thousands of years ago, the creature and its famous Labyrinth have continued to fascinate people, as shown by the drawings, statues, and other depictions of the monster.

MINOTAUR

CHAPTER 5

The Meaning of the Minotaur

The Minotaur myth was extremely important to the ancient Greeks, and especially to the citizens of Athens. In Greek, the word *Minotaur* is *Minotauros,* which is a combination of *Minos* and *tauros:* "the bull of Minos."

According to Finley Hooper in the book *Greek Realities,* very early in Greek history, Attica—the southern part of Greece that contains Athens and juts into the Aegean Sea—was composed of a number of small communities, each ruled by a monarch. Eventually a king managed to unite all of these communities into the single entity of Athens. Theseus is most often given credit for doing this. Once the small kingdoms were united into a strong whole, they were tough enough to resist powerful Crete, which had been forcing their young men to serve in Crete's navy. Thus the tale of the Minotaur may be seen as an allegory: The Minotaur represents Crete stealing the youths of Attica, and Theseus stops this plundering by killing the creature—just as the uniting of the kingdoms stopped the practice.[1]

According to Robert Graves, the sacrifice of the seven Athenian male youths actually goes back to a real-life practice that saw youths sacrificed for their king. It is possible that this custom was used in Crete. However, instead of sacrificing native people from Crete, youths from other areas—such as Athens—were likely substituted. Graves goes on to say that the seven females from Athens were not sacrificed. Rather, it is possible that they became attendants for Cretan priests of a moon goddess. They may have even performed a type of gymnastics as entertainment at bullfights.[2]

What makes it difficult to definitively choose a theory or idea is that we know very little about the civilization on ancient Crete. A good deal of what we know comes from faded images painted on broken pieces of pottery discovered during archaeological excavations—not exactly the best way to try to understand a sophisticated ancient civilization.

The civilization that arose on Crete is known as the Minoan civilization (after King Minos). It is thought that the Minoans worshiped goddesses, rather than male gods. Even though bulls are male, they seem to have played a major role in Minoan religion. There are images of bulls and of bull horns in the pottery discovered from ancient Crete. Thus, in a broad sense, the death of the Minotaur by Theseus can be seen as the replacement—or death—of the female-oriented Minoan religion by that of the male-dominated religion of Athens as represented by Zeus (Theseus).

Graves identifies one of the main goddesses in the Minoan religion as Ariadne—the same as the princess who helped Theseus. He says that Ariadne is the daughter (or younger self) of an ancient goddess of Crete—Pasiphae (who was the mother of the Minotaur).[3] Graves also notes: "It is evident from the legends . . . that male human sacrifice was an integral part of her [Ariadne] worship."[4]

Could this be the origin of the Minotaur myth? Can this explain the battle between Theseus and the Minotaur?

Sleeping Ariadne, by Cornielle Van Clève

Other evidence from faded wall paintings indicates that men, women, and bulls danced together somehow in ancient Crete, in a form of ritual. As myth scholar Alexander Eliot notes: "The most astonishing and famous of [the images] seems to depict athletes leaping across the horns of a bull."[5]

Some experts have theorized that the story of the Minotaur actually has its roots in a celebration, complete with ritual dancing. Wouldn't it be ironic if the story of the Minotaur is not actually about death, but about dancing?

These images raise the possibility that what went on in the Labyrinth was not deadly, but perhaps entertaining. As Eliot states: "In fact it may have been not so much a murderous struggle between man and beast as a deliberate expression of amity [friendship] in power—an admittedly dangerous but harmonious dancing of young men and women with the mighty bulls."[6]

The Minotaur on the Shattered Cliff, by Gustave Doré for Dante's *Inferno*. In the *Inferno* (which is Italian for "hell"), Dante imagines the suffering of the Minotaur after its death.

Could this be true? Is the real story behind the Minotaur not one of death, but of life? Were people not dying, but dancing?

It is perhaps foolish to base such complex theories about the Labyrinth and the Minotaur on faded images thousands of years old. But the paintings provide a starting point for understanding Minoan civilization.

As far as the Labyrinth itself, the word means "the house of labrys." A *lavrys* is a double-edged ax—a symbol of the ancient Minoan religion, much as the cross is a symbol of Christianity. It has

An ancient Mosaic in Paphos, Cyprus, depicts a labyrinth leading to the Minotaur, Theseus, Ariadne, Daedalus, and Icarus in the center.

been found inscribed in many objects and buildings of the ancient Minoans.[7] It is very possible that something like the Labyrinth actually existed, because of the importance of the labrys to the Minoans.

When modern archaeologists discovered the palace of King Minos, it was suggested that the palace itself was the actual Labyrinth. For years that theory was believed, but the idea has fallen into disfavor.

Another idea has resurfaced that was apparently commonplace in earlier times: The Labyrinth is a maze-like cave in Messara in the Gortys area south of Heraklion in Crete.[8] According to Greek scholars Kaloust Paragamian and Antonis Vasilakis, during the fourteenth to seventeenth centuries, governors of the island nation would visit a large quarry located in Ambelouzos, because they believed the mythical Labyrinth was located there. As war spread across the world during the twentieth century, people sometimes took refuge in this area to escape the fighting.

Indeed, during World War II a portion of this cave was used by the occupying German army as a munitions dump. As they were preparing to evacuate it, the German army blew it up so that the Allied forces would not take control of it. This explosion destroyed several areas of the Labyrinth and seriously weakened others to the point that they may yet fall.[9]

Could this natural area be the source of the Labyrinth myth, and that of the Minotaur? Or could the palace of King Minos actually be the Labyrinth? Or is there another explanation?

Much of the history of ancient Greece and related civilizations remains hidden. It is likely that the true story of the hideous man-beast the Minotaur and his home the Labyrinth still lies buried somewhere, waiting to be discovered. Only then will the actual meaning of Theseus, Minos, Ariadne, Daedalus, and the Minotaur come to light. Perhaps the person who will discover the truth is reading this book right now.

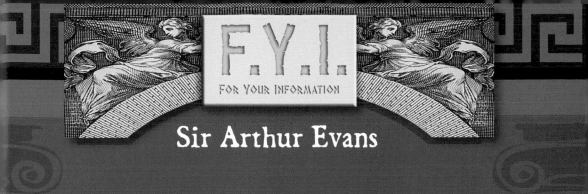
Sir Arthur Evans

Arthur Evans will forever hold a place in archaeological history because of his discovery of Knossos, the ancient palace of King Minos on the island of Crete.

Evans was born in Nash Mills, England, on July 8, 1851, to John Evans and Harriet Ann Dickerson. From 1884 to 1908, he was the curator of the Ashmolean Museum of Art and Archeology at Oxford, England.

It had long been known that an ancient civilization existed in the area south of Heraklion in Crete. Local inhabitants would often unearth historical objects as they worked in the fields. It is one of the curious accidents of history that Evans wound up getting the archaeological credit.

The first person to excavate the area was Minos Kalokairinos, a lover of ancient civilizations. In 1878 he uncovered two of the storerooms of King Minos's palace. However, the owners of the land forced him to stop his work. Archaeologist Heinrich Schliemann, who had also searched for Troy, attempted to purchase the land, but could not because the price was too high.

Thus it fell to Evans to make this amazing find. Evans knew of the importance of the area. He had been trying to decipher some of the writing found on stones there, so he was in a perfect position to make his move in 1900, after Crete became an independent nation. He bought the land from the new owners and quickly began excavations.

Very soon Evans uncovered King Minos's palace. When he discovered thousands of clay tablets with writing, he concluded that an ancient civilization had indeed existed there. He also found evidence that the people had worshiped bulls. In honor of King Minos, Evans called the civilization the Minoan Civilization.

When Evans uncovered the ruins of Knossos, it had a maze-like quality to it, with many levels. It reminded him of the Labyrinth of Greek legend, thus spawning the idea that the king's palace was the actual Labyrinth.

Evans finished his excavations in 1905 and was knighted in 1911 for his contributions to archaeology. He published his findings in four volumes entitled *The Palace of Minos at Knossos*. He died in 1941.

Chapter One. Hunting Evil

1. Greeka: "Ancient Crete: The Glorious History of Minoan Crete, Greece," http://www.greeka.com/crete/crete-history/ancient-crete.htm

Chapter Two. The Tale of Two Kings

1. Robert Graves, *The Greek Myths* (London, England: Penguin Books, 1992), p. 292.
2. Ibid.
3. Ibid.
4. Ibid.
5. Félix Guirand, *Greek Mythology* (London: Batchworth Press Limited, 1963), p. 150.
6. Graves, p. 293.
7. Ron Leadbetter, "Minos," *Encyclopedia Mythica,* 1999, http://www.pantheon.org/articles/m/minos.html
8. Graves, p. 293.
9. Ibid.
10. Ibid., p. 294.
11. Ibid.

Chapter Three. Theseus the Hero

1. Lucilla Burn, *Greek Myths* (Austin: University of Texas Press, 1990), p. 25.
2. Edith Hamilton, *Mythology* (New York: New American Library, 1989), p. 150.
3. Burn, p. 27.
4. Hamilton, p. 150.
5. Félix Guirand, *Greek Mythology* (London: Batchworth Press Limited, 1963), p. 150.
6. Ibid.
7. Padraic Colum, *The Golden Fleece and the Heroes Who Lived before Achilles* (New York: The Macmillan Co., 1922; New York: Bartleby.com, 2000), http://www.bartleby.com/72/33.html

Chapter Four. Fight to the Death!

1. Donald Richardson, *Great Zeus and All His Children* (Columbus, OH: Greyden Press), p. 146.

2. Ibid.
3. Edith Hamilton, *Mythology* (New York: New American Library, 1989), p. 149.
4. Arthur Cotterell, *The Minoan World* (New York: Charles Scribner's Sons, 1979), p. 110.
5. Ibid.
6. Ibid., p. 111.

Chapter Five. The Meaning of the Minotaur

1. Finley Hooper, *Greek Realities* (New York: Charles Scribner's Sons, 1967), p. 134.
2. Robert Graves, *The Greek Myths* (London: Penguin Books, 1992), p. 311.
3. Robert Graves, *The White Goddess* (New York: Farrar, Straus, and Giroux, 1948), p. 99.
4. Ibid.
5. Alexander Eliot, *The Horizon Concise History of Greece* (New York: American Heritage Publishing Co., Inc., 1972), p. 19.
6. Ibid.
7. "The Labyrinth of Crete: The Myth of Minotaur," from *The Labyrinth of Messara* by Kaloust Paragamian and Antonis Vasilakis; English translation by Lou Duro for ExploreCrete.com, http://www.explorecrete.com/history/labyrinthmyth.htm
8. Ibid.
9. Ibid.

**The Minotaur
and the Hare,
by Sopie
Ryder**

For Young Adults

Byrd, Robert. *The Hero and the Minotaur: The Fantastic Adventures of Theseus*. New York: Dutton's Children's Books, 2005.

Green, Jen. *Myths of Ancient Greece*. Austin, Texas: Raintree Steck-Vaughn, 2001.

Houle, Michelle M. *Gods and Goddesses in Greek Mythology*. Berkeley Heights, New Jersey: Enslow Publishers, 2001.

McCarty, Nick. *The Iliad*. Boston: Kingfisher, 2004.

McGee, Marni, *Ancient Greece: Archeology Unlocks the Secrets of Greece's Past*. Washington, D.C.: National Geographic, 2007.

Schulte, Mary. *The Minotaur*. Farmington Hills, Michigan: Kidhaven Press, 2008.

Weber, Belinda. *The Best Book of Ancient Greece*. New York: Kingfisher, 2005.

Works Consulted

Avery, Catherine B., editor. *The New Century Handbook of Greek Mythology and Legend*. New York: Meredith Corporation, 1972.

Burn, Lucilla. *Greek Myths*. Austin: University of Texas Press, 1990.

Colum, Padraic. *The Golden Fleece and the Heroes Who Lived before Achilles*. New York: The Macmillan Co., 1922; New York: Bartleby.com, 2000. http://www.bartleby.com/72/

Cotterell, Arthur. *The Minoan World*. New York: Charles Scribner's Sons, 1979.

Eliot, Alexander. *The Horizon Concise History of Greece*. New York: American Heritage Publishing Co., Inc., 1972.

Garland, Robert. *Daily Life of the Ancient Greeks*. Westport, Connecticut: Greenwood Press, 1998.

Graves, Robert. *The Greek Myths*. London: Penguin Books, 1992.

——. *The White Goddess*. New York: Farrar, Straus, and Giroux, 1948.

Guirand, Félix. *Greek Mythology*. London: Batchworth Press Limited, 1963.

Hamilton, Edith. *Mythology*. New York: New American Library, 1989.

Hooper, Finley. *Greek Realities*. New York: Charles Scribner's Sons, 1967.

Martin, Thomas R. *Ancient Greece*. New Haven, Connecticut: Yale University Press, 1996.

Paragamian, Kaloust, and Antonis Vasilakis. *The Labyrinth of Messara*. English translation by Lou Duro for ExploreCrete.com, http://www.explorecrete.com/history/labyrinth-myth.htm

Richardson, Donald, *Great Zeus and All His Children*. Columbus, Ohio: Greyden Press, 1993.

On the Internet
Ancient Greece
    http://ancient-greece.org/
Ancient Greece
    http://www.ancientgreece.com/s/Main_Page
Ancient Greece for Kids
    http://greece.mrdonn.org/
History Link 101: Ancient Greece
    http://www.historylink101.com/ancient_greece.htm
Kidipede: Ancient Greece
    http://www.historyforkids.org/learn/greeks/
Leadbetter, Ron: *Encyclopedia Mythica*
    www.pantheon.org

GLOSSARY

accede (ak-SEED)—To approve or agree to something; to take an office.

allegory (AL-eh-gor-ee)—A tale whose parts represent real-life people or events.

appall (ah-PAWL)—To fill with horror or dismay.

contradict (kon-trah-DIKT)—To say two things that are opposites.

excavate (EX-kuh-vayt)—To expose by digging.

hereditary (huh-REH-dih-tayr-ee)—Passing from parents to children.

kylix (KY-liks)—An ancient Greek drinking cup with two handles and a wide, shallow bowl.

loathsome (LOWTH-sum)—Disgusting.

mutant (MYOO-tunt)—A new kind of organism based on an established one.

renown (ree-NOWN)—Fame.

ruffian (RUH-fee-un)—A brutal bully.

surly (SIR-lee)—Bad-tempered.

tribute (TRIB-yoot)—A gift of gratitude.

vindictive (vin-DIK-tiv)—Seeking revenge.

INDEX